ROMAN ROADS
OF
KENT

Alex Vincent

MP Middleton Press

Overall cover (front and back) - Richborough to Dover Roman road along a footpath west of Guston.

Front cover (inset) - Richborough to Dover Roman road at Cane Wood, near Pineham.

Back cover (inset) - Roman road (Stone Street) ascending a hill, south of Canterbury.

Published April 2007

ISBN 978 1 906008 02 4

© Middleton Press, 2007

Design Deborah Esher

Published by
Middleton Press
Easebourne Lane
Midhurst
West Sussex
GU29 9AZ
Tel: 01730 813169
Fax: 01730 812601
Email: info@middletonpress.co.uk
www.middletonpress.co.uk

Printed & bound by Biddles Ltd, Kings Lynn

CONTENTS

ACKNOWLEDGEMENTS

I wish to thank the staff of Kent Archaeological Society, Kent Record Office, various libraries, museums and many other people for their help in preparing this book. Mr D and Dr S Salter have kindly proof read the text. The Fleur de Lis Heritage Centre in Faversham has also been of great assistance.

By the same author -

Roman Roads of Hampshire
Roman Roads of Surrey
Roman Roads of Sussex

1. INTRODUCTION

There were some 10,000 miles of Roman roads in Britain of which about 7500 miles are known, with another 2500 or so yet to be proved and possibly many more still to be discovered. Most construction of Roman roads was done during the first century AD. Some of these roads were military, some for commercial use and others were purely local.

Roman roads were mainly built straight, but not from start to finish as there were changes in direction en-route particularly where they descended hills on terraceways. Purely local Roman roads were not necessarily straight and where the terrain was very hilly with steep sided valleys, a straight road would not be possible and would have to have curves in many places. Many Roman roads joined and crossed each other in cities, but some junctions were in the countryside.

Width and surfaces of roads varied a great deal from one region to another. Most main Roman roads were 20 – 23 feet wide, but could have been more if traffic was heavier. Most were on an agger or embankment, with ditches on either side. Materials used on roads depended on what was available in the area. Chalk and flint for example was used in southern England and Limestone in the north and west. Most Roman roads were paved.

There were no paved roads in Britain, apart from a few timbered causeways, before the Roman period. Not all Roman roads were paved because if the soil was well drained then paving would not have been necessary and this also applies to purely local roads as well. The soil from cuttings would have been used for embankments.

Roman roads were built to give access to the Roman settlements across Britain and to connect towns and cities. Some were provided with posting stations or mansios, which were placed at intervals of between 12 and 15 miles, as this represented a day's travelling. Posting stations consisted of an embanked area some 2½ to 4 acres in a rectangle. They comprised an inn, stables and a few houses.

Roman roads crossed rivers, streams and estuaries by means of either a bridge, ford or ferry. The Romans preferred to ford and those on foot had wet feet, whilst some waded up to their waist. Some fords were paved such as at Iden Green in Kent. An estuary was crossed by a ferry, as were the Rivers Adur and Arun in Sussex. Other waterways were crossed by a bridge where wooden piles were driven into a river bed, such as at Alfoldean on Stane Street in Sussex.

A great number of Roman roads are still visible today either as an agger (embankment), hollow way (cutting), a terraceway on a hill, simply hedgerows or treelines. Footpaths and modern roads also mark their course. Others are not visible above ground due to erosion, extensive ploughing or developments such as housing. Those not visible on the ground may sometimes be seen from the air and aerial photography has revealed many sites.

Mr I.D. Margary (1896 – 1976) specialised in the study of Roman roads. He discovered the line of a Roman road, between Chuck Hatch near Hartfield and Camp Hill near Duddleswell, on aerial photographs, which were taken of the Ashdown Forest in 1929. This was the London to Lewes Roman road and after this, Margary visited all known sites throughout the country. He wrote a number of books and many articles recording his findings. He gave all Roman roads reference numbers from Watling Street (No. 1), Ermine Street (No. 2), The Great Road (No. 3) and so on.

Where the Roman road was long, it is divided by letters in the lower case such as Watling Street, (Dover to Wroxeter), where the section from Dover to Canterbury is Margary's No. 1a, Canterbury to Rochester No. 1b, Rochester to London 1c etc. These numbers are used throughout this book.

There are many names that can suggest a Roman route, such as Street, Streat, Streatham, Stratton, Stratford, Coldharbour and Wickham. Also Ridgeway, Causeway, Green Street, Folly

Hill and Ford names are worth looking into. Names like Stan, Stane, Stanstead, Strett and Stone may have derived from the stony nature of a Roman road. Places in Britain with these names may well occur near or on the line of a possible Roman road.

This book gives details of all the Roman roads in Kent, starting with its title, Margary number, length in miles, description of the route, maps and photographs (taken by the author). There are 13 of them and at the end of the book is a section on other Roman roads, which may exist as well as other tracks, which are dotted all over the county.

The Ordnance Survey maps herein are at the scale of 1 ins to 1 mile and north is at the top, except where rotation of the place names indicates otherwise. They were all published in the late 1940s, when there was less building development to hinder the study of Roman roads. Many of their alignments are marked thereon, as understood at that time. The existence of a footpath on these maps does not necessarily indicate a right of way and thus current maps and signposts are needed to determine this fact. Many of the locations described are on private property and consent must be obtained before entering onto such land. The recent "Right to Roam" legislation has many limitations and is not what its popular title suggests. The numbers in black circles on the maps indicate the locations of the relevant photographs.

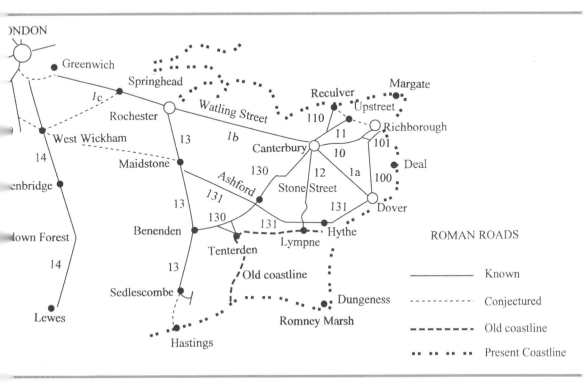

2. DOVER TO CANTERBURY (Watling Street)
(1a) 14 miles

Watling Street is the most famous of Roman roads in Britain. It went from Dover in Kent to the Roman town of Viroconium at Wroxeter in Shropshire, via London, Verulamium at St Albans, and Towcester. This Roman road was known as Casingc or Key Street in Saxon times and the name exists today in a hamlet called "Key Street" west of Sittingbourne in Kent. The name Watling Street came later.

It left the Roman town of Dubris in Dover, (which was around the market square), and went in a north-westerly direction running along a precinct, then the A256 main road to Buckland and Oldpark Hill. After this, the route ran along the B2060 at Kearsney, through Temple Ewell, (where there is a bend), to Lydden. At the latter place, the Roman road descended Lydden Hill in a hollow way west of the B2060, which is marked by a treeline at Bell Farm Lydden, and through Lyddenhill Wood.

North of Lydden, the route is marked by a treeline east of the main A2 past Ropersole Farm, through Wick Wood, and Denne Hill. After this, the Roman road crossed the A2 east of Barham and ran west of it over Barham Downs, and to the east of Bishopsbourne. North of this, the Roman road went along the High Street through the village of Bridge to Remville Farm. From here, the A2050 marks its course for about half a mile, and then along the Old Dover Road. It then entered the Roman town of Durovernum at Canterbury at the Ridingate.

***2.1. Watling Street entering the Roman town of Dubris along
Cannon Street (now a precinct) in Dover***

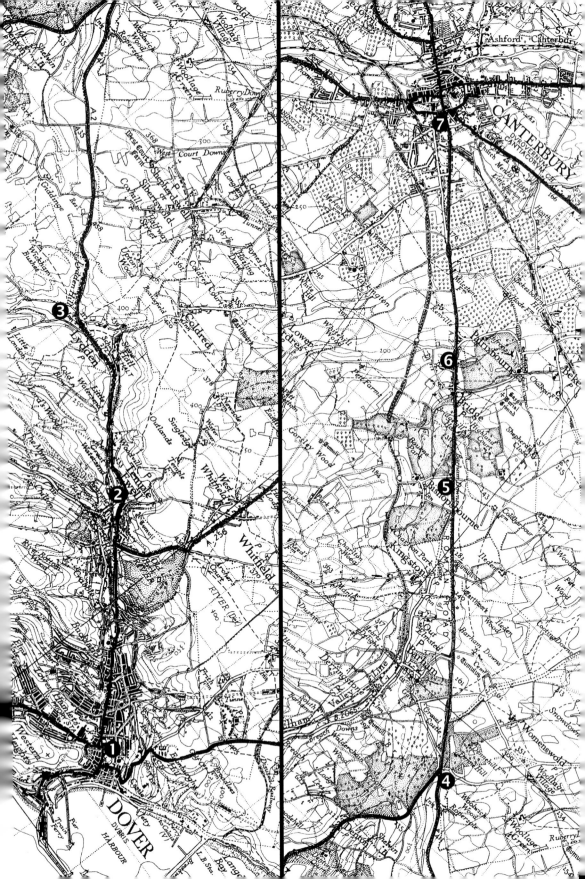

2.2. Watling Street along the B2060 in Temple Ewell.

2.3. Watling Street marked as a treeline at Lydden.

2.4. Watling Street along a treeline at Denne Hill near Womenswold.

2.5. The line of Watling Street west of the A2 over Barham Downs.

2.6. Watling Street along the High Street through the village of Bridge.

2.7. Watling Street entering the Roman town of
Durovernum in Canterbury at the Ridingate.

3. CANTERBURY TO ROCHESTER. (Watling Street)
(1b). 25 ½ miles

This section of Watling Street left the Roman town of Durovernum, at the West Gate, and continued in a north-westerly direction along the A290 to St Dunstan's church. From here, the Roman road changed direction along a minor road through Harbledown, then along the A2 to Dunkirk, where a minor road marks its course to Boughton Street and Nash Court. The route is then marked by the A2 again from Brenley Corner, Preston and through the southern part of Faversham.

West of Faversham, the Roman road continued along the A2 through Ospringe, Syndale and Stone where the Roman town of Durolevum stood. The ruined Stone chapel incorporates parts of a Roman temple. A strip of country between Faversham and Stone is rich in Roman remains. West of Stone, the Roman road ran along the A2 through Teynham, Bapchild, Sittingbourne, Key Street (named from the Roman road), Newington, Gillingham and Chatham. The route then entered the Roman town of Durobrivae, (Rochester), at the East Gate where it is marked by the High Street.

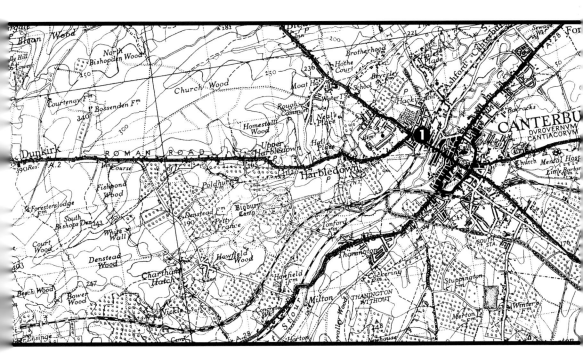

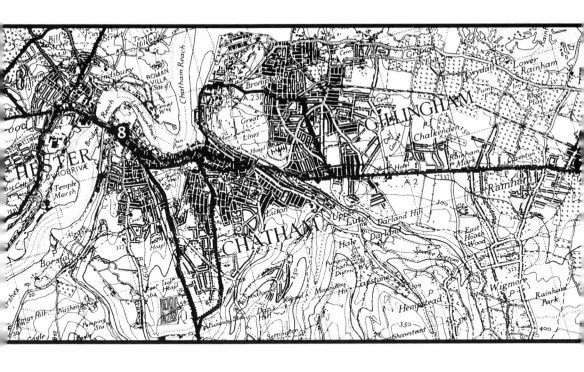

3.1. Watling Street along St Dunstan's Street as it leaves Canterbury at the West Gate.

3.2.   Watling Street along Canterbury Road through the village of Boughton Street.

3.3.   Watling Street along the A2 through Faversham.

3.4. Watling Street along the A2 at Beacon Hill, Stone at the site of the Roman town of Durolevum.

3.5. Watling Street along a precinct through the town of Sittingbourne.

3.6. Watling Street through Key Street, which was named from the Roman road.

3.7. Watling Street along the High Street at Rainham.

3.8. Watling Street along the High street, Rochester in the Roman town of Durobrivae.

4. ROCHESTER TO LONDON. (Watling Street)
(1c). 28 ¾ miles

This section of Watling Street left the Roman town of Durobrivae at Rochester at the West Gate. It went in a westerly direction and crossed the River Medway on a bridge, (site now occupied by the present road and railway bridge). Wooden piles of this bridge were found in the 19th century. West of the river crossing, the Roman road crossed a marsh to Strood Hill on a causeway, which was about 375 yards long.

The Roman road then ran along the A2 through Strood, and slightly south of it at Cobham Park. It then ran along a minor road called "Watling Street" through Singlewell. West of this, the route ran along or near the A2 main road to Springhead, where there is the site of a sizeable Roman town called "Vagniacae". This is situated in a field south of the main road. The Roman road then continued along the A2 to Stonewood, where it changed direction to the north-west, along the A296 and B2500 to Dartford.

The Roman road went past the parish church and along a precinct in Dartford. There was a Roman cemetery here. After Dartford, the route ran along the A207 through Crayford, Bexley (where it is marked by a treeline), Welling, Shooters Hill, Eltham Common on a treeline and to the north of Kidbrooke. Here the B211 marks it to Greenwich where it changed direction to the south-west along Charlton Way north of Blackheath. From here the Roman road went through Deptford and New Cross to the Roman bridge over the Thames, (just east of the present London Bridge), to the Roman town of Londinium.

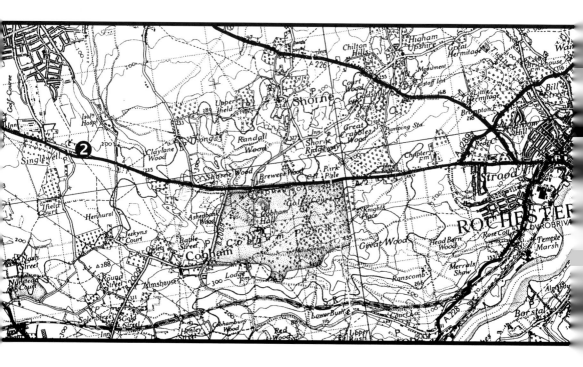

4.1. Site of Roman bridge, which carried Watling Street over the River Medway in Rochester.

4.2.   The line of Watling Street along a minor road called Watling Street at Singlewell.

4.3. Site of Watling Street at the Roman town of Vagnacae at Springhead.

4.4. Watling Street through the town of Dartford.

4.5. Watling Street along London Road at Crayford.

4.6. Watling Street marked as a treeline in Bexley.

4.7. Watling Street along the A207 in Shooters Hill.

4.8. Watling Street along Charlton Way north of Blackheath looking towards London.

5. CANTERBURY TO RICHBOROUGH
(10) 11 ½ miles

This Roman road left the Roman town of Durovernum at Canterbury at the Bargate. It went eastwards along the A257 near the Saxon church of St Martin, (built on the site of a Roman one), and then along the A257 from St Martin's Hill to Littlebourne. Here the route goes across a field and through Pine Wood north of the main road. It then ran along the A257 again through Littlebourne, to Bramling where a minor road marks its course to Neavy Downs via Wingham Well.

From here, the Roman road changed direction along the B2046 to Wingham, and then along the A257 through the village. After this, the route turned eastwards along the main road through Shatterling and Ash. At the latter place, the Roman road turned to the north-east along a footpath to Cooper Street and across a field to Fleet Farm. The Roman road crossed an estuary here on a causeway to Richborough Hill where there is a cutting. It then went past Richborough Farm, along a minor road, footpath and then entered the Roman port of Rutupiae at Richborough.

This was the first Roman road to be built in Britain, and was probably an important route because the port at Rutupiae was a principal entry from Gaul. The port started in 43 AD and was believed to be an extensive town. The Saxon Shore fort was erected on the site in about 280-90 AD. It was surrounded on three sides by water when built, but due to the Wantsum Channel silting up, it is now about two miles inland. The fort exists today as ruins and earthworks.

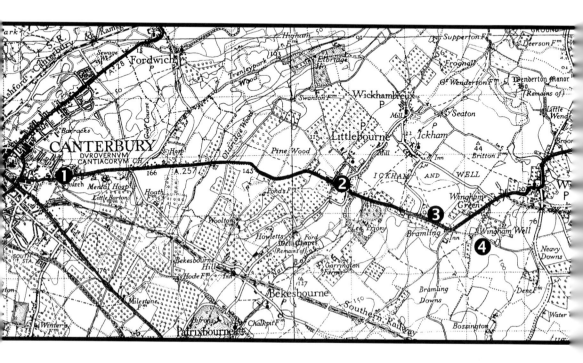

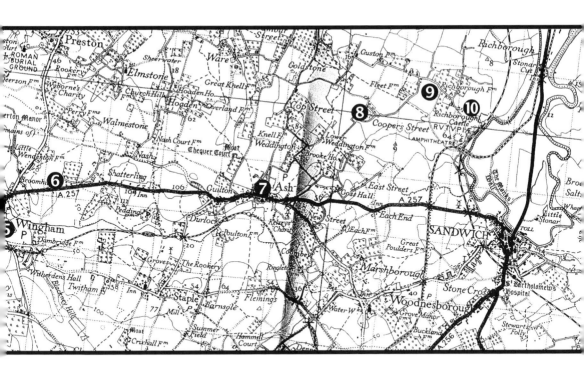

5.1 The Canterbury to Richborough Roman road along the A257 in Canterbury.

5.2 The Roman road along the A257 through the village of Littlebourne.

5.3. The route along the main road through Bramling.

5.4. The Roman road along a minor road at Wingham Well.

5.5. The line of the Roman road through the village of Wingham.

5.6. The straightness of the Roman road along the A257 west of Shatterling.

5.7. The route through the village of Ash.

5.8. The Roman road along a footpath at Cooper Street.

5.9. The Roman road on Richborough Hill as a cutting and site of causeway to Fleet Farm.

5.10. The Canterbury to Richborough Roman road along a footpath to the Roman port of Rutupiae at Richborough Castle.

6. CANTERBURY TO UPSTREET
(11) 15 miles

This Roman road left Canterbury at the North Gate and went in a north-easterly direction along the A28 main road to Sturry. It is marked by a treeline and went to the north of Sturry church after crossing the Great Stour River. It is possible that the Roman road ran along a footpath south of the A28 to Fordwich instead. At Fordwich, the route would have turned north along a footpath and minor road, crossing the Great Stour there, and then the A28 marks its course to Sturry.

At Sturry, the Roman road continued to the north-east along the A28 where the Sturry to Reculver Roman road (Margary's No 110) branched off some ¾ mile further east. After this, route 11 went through Westbere, Hersden, and then to Upstreet. The Roman road is mainly raised throughout its course and there is a bend in it at Upstreet to avoid low ground. The route went through the village of Upstreet. This Roman road was known as "Dunstret" in 1414.

After Upstreet, the A28 is on the Sarre Wall, and this is where a possible ferry may have existed to the Isle of Thanet, which was an island in Roman times. This estuary was known as the Wantsum Channel and the crossing would have been 1½ miles wide. It is possible that the Roman road continued eastwards from Sarre, Monkton, and beyond to Margate or Ramsgate, serving Roman settlements en-route.

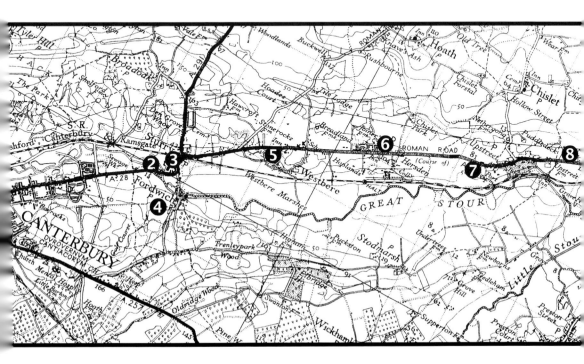

6.1. The Canterbury to Upstreet Roman road entering the Roman town of Durovernum at the North Gate in Canterbury.

6.2. Possible route of the Roman road along a treeline in Sturry.

6.3. Possible line of the route to the north of Sturry church.

6.4. Alternative route of the Roman road as a possible agger in a field at Fordwich.

6.5. The route along the A28 in Westbere.

6.6. The route along the main road in Hersden.

6.7. The Roman road along the A28 through Upstreet where there is a bend to avoid low ground.

6.8 Possible route of the Canterbury to Upstreet Roman road east of Upstreet where there may have been a causeway to the Isle of Thanet.

7. CANTERBURY TO LYMPNE. (Stone Street) (12). 15 miles

This Roman road known as "Stone Street" left Canterbury at the Worth Gate and went southwards to Lympne. Leyland called it a "Fayr paved road". It is marked by the A28 for a short distance where the Benenden to Canterbury Roman road (Margary's No. 130) branched off. The first mile of the route to Lympne is not known, but could be along a footpath where it ascends a hill to Stubbington.

South of Stubbington, the Roman road ran along Iffin Lane from Stubbington Farm, past Iffin's Farm to Harmansole Farm west of Lower Hadres. From here, the route ran on a straight alignment just west of the B2068 through Petham, and then along the road from Little Wadden Hall, west of Stelling Minnis, Maxted Street, Lymbridge Green, Stowting and Stanford. At Petham, high ground was made use of and south of Stowting, the route makes a bend at Farthing Corner to avoid low ground.

At Stanford, the Roman road ran along a minor road through the village. South of this, the M20 motorway has obliterated it, but then another minor road marks it through Westenhanger. It then ran across a field to Lympne, crossing the Maidstone to Dover Roman road (Margary's No. 131) at Shepway Cross and ran along Lympne Hill to west Hythe where a combe provided an easy descent to the Roman port of Portus Lemanis. The site is probably situated east of the road, north of West Hythe Bridge, on the Royal Military Canal.

A section of Stone Street also ran along Stone Street on the B2068, which is thought to be a later diversion of the Roman road to Lympne castle. The Roman fort at Stutfall castle was built in about 280 AD, and was one of the forts of the Saxon shore. It was on the coast, but due to silting up of the coast, it is now about 1½ miles inland. There are scattered ruins of the fort on the hillside near a footpath. It is possible that the Romans built another fort in around 370 AD further north, but no evidence of this has been found. The site is probably in the vicinity of the present village and castle at Lympne.

7.1. Stone Street along Castle Street in the Roman town of Durovernum in Canterbury.

7.2. Stone Street ascending a hill along a footpath south of Canterbury.

7.3. Stone Street along Iffin Lane at Iffin's Farm near Stubbington.

7.4. Stone Street along a treeline at the back of a pub in Petham.

7.5. Stone Street along the B2068 road near Stelling Minnis.

7.6. Stone Street along the B2068 at Sixmile near Lymbridge Green.

7.7. Stone Street along the B2068 where it bends at Farthing Corner.

7.8. Stone Street along a minor road through Stanford.

7.9. Stone Street where it crosses the Maidstone to Dover Roman road at Shepway Cross near Lympne.

7.10. Stone Street along Lympne Hill to the possible site of the Roman port of Portus Lemanis at West Hythe.

8. ROCHESTER TO HASTINGS
(13). 37 miles

This Roman road branched off Watling Street (Margary's No. 1b) near the junction of Delce Road and Star Hill in Rochester. It went in a southerly direction along City Road and Williams Way in Rochester, and then the A229 marks its course to Bluebell Hill. From here, the route is marked by a minor road to Kits Coty, and then along a footpath, and another minor road to Tyland Farm. South of this, the Roman road runs along or near the A229 main road to Maidstone.

At Maidstone, the route is marked by Sandling Road, Week Street (now a precinct), Gabriel's Hill, Lower Stone Street, Upper Stone Street, and then along Loose Road. South of this, the Roman road ran through a cemetery, along a hedgerow at the edge of a park, and then a treelined footpath marks its course for a while. From here, a minor road marks the route to Park Wood and then it goes through Horsted where the Maidstone to Dover Roman road (Margary's No. 131) branched off.

South of Horsted, the route ran along a minor road through Rabbit's Cross and crossed the River Beult east of Cross at Hand. From here, the Roman road ran along the A229 through Staplehurst for a couple of miles, passing Knox Bridge, and then through Sissinghurst and Golford, (where it bends), and then to Benenden. At the latter place, the Benenden to Canterbury Roman road (Margary's No. 130) joined it. Just south of Benenden, the Roman road crossed a stream on a paved ford at Iden Green, where there are still some rocks, east of Stream Farm.

After Iden Green, the route went through Eaglesden along a minor road to Sandhurst where it ran over a hill on a footpath to Sandhurst Cross. After this, the route entered Sussex and went to Hastings via Bodiam (where it crossed the River Rother on a causeway or ferry), Staple Cross, Sedlescombe and Westfield. It possibly went to the iron working site at Beaufort Park north of Hastings, and possibly joined a ridgeway at Ore.

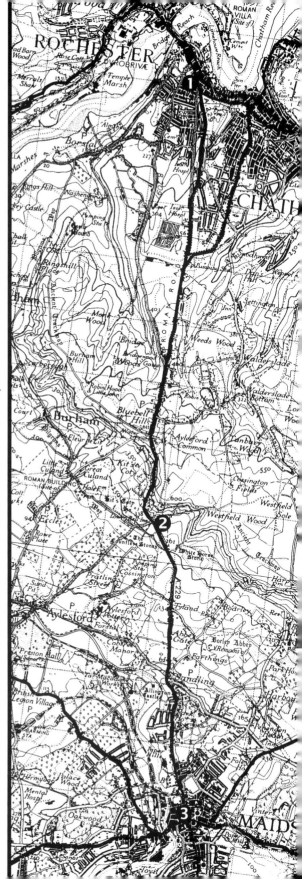

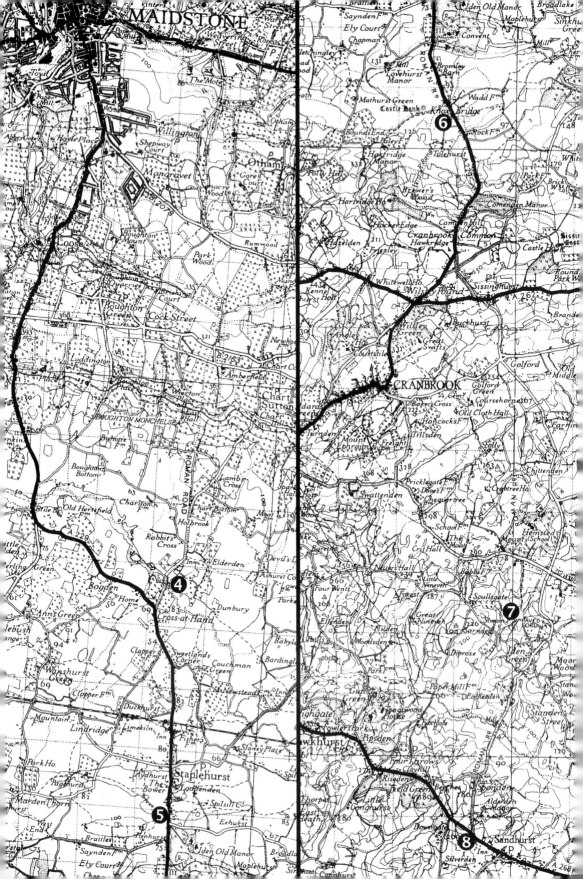

8.1. The Rochester to Hastings Roman road along Delce Road in Rochester.

8.2. The route marked by a footpath at Kits Coty.

8.3. The Roman road along Week Street in Maidstone.

8.4. The route marked by a treeline at Rabbit's Cross.

8.5. The line of the Roman road along the A229 main road through Staplehurst.

8.6. The straightness of the Roman road along the A229 at Knox Bridge.

8.7. Site of the paved ford on the Roman road at Stream Farm, Iden Green.

8.8. Site of the Rochester to Hastings Roman road along hedgerows at Sandhurst.

9. LONDON TO LEWES
(14). 44 miles

This Roman road was built to serve the iron working area of the Weald and the corn growing regions of the South Downs. It branched off Watling Street (Margary's No. 1c) at Peckham and went in a south-easterly direction through Nunhead, (along a treeline), Beckenham and West Wickham, where it is marked by trees. At West Wickham in fields west of the church is the site of the Roman town of Noviomagus, where artifacts have been found.

South of West Wickham, the Roman road is marked by trees and ran along the Kent/Surrey border at New Addington. The route then ran along Skid Hill Lane for about a mile, and turned to the south-east in a V shape to cross a deep valley at Skid Hill, which exists today as a terraceway. From here, the Roman road continued along the Kent/Surrey border through Mollards Wood, and west of Tatsfield where there is a terraceway, and through Titsey in Surrey.

At Titsey, the Roman road crossed the M25 near the Clacket Lane service station, where there are artifacts on display from the nearby excavated Roman villa and temple. South of the M25, the route ran east of Titsey Wood, through The High Chart, and entered Kent at Kent Hatch near Crockham Hill. The Roman road ran along a minor road in Crockham Hill and then across fields east of the B2026 to Marlpit Hill. At the latter place, the route ran along the B2026 and through the town of Edenbridge. South of the town, it crossed the River Eden on a causeway.

South of Edenbridge, the Roman road is marked by a lane and footpath east of Marsh Green to Cobhambury Farm, and through Ludwells Farm, passing west of Cowden along a treeline and entered Sussex at Holtye, where there is a preserved section, which was excavated in 1939. South of this, the route ran across the Ashdown Forest, and changed direction to the south-west, going through Duddleswell, Maresfield, Isfield, Barcombe Mills, and then ascended Malling Hill, Lewes where it connected with other trackways.

9.1. The London to Lewes Roman road marked by trees at Nunhead.

9.2. The Roman road marked by hedgerows at the site of the Roman town of Noviomagus at West Wickham.

9.3. The route as a terraceway along the Kent/Surrey border on Skid Hill.

9.4. The road at Kent Hatch north of Crockham Hill.

9.5. The Roman road along a minor road through Crockham Hill.

9.6.   The route along the B2026 road at Marlpit Hill north of Edenbridge.

9.7.   The Roman road along the High Street through the town of Edenbridge.

9.8. The road along a lane east of Marsh Green.

9.9. Site of the Roman road across a field at Cobhambury Farm.

9.10. The London to Lewes Roman road marked by a treeline west of Cowden.

10. RICHBOROUGH TO DOVER
(100). 10 ¾ miles

This Roman road left the Canterbury to Richborough route (Margary's No. 10) at Ash some 200 yards or so east of the church. It ran along a footpath where there is an agger going in a south-easterly direction. It then went along a minor road through Coombe and followed a footpath near Marshborough, and then another minor road marks it to Woodnesborough, where Roman road No. 101 joined it from Sandwich just north of the church.

South of Woodnesborough, the Roman road ran along Foxborough Hill to Eastry and through this village along the High Street, then Lower Street. From Woodnesborough, this Roman road ran almost due south on a straight alignment to Dover. From Eastry, the route continued along the minor road for about a mile and then a footpath marks its course from Betteshanger to Telegraph Farm near Tilmanstone. South of the farm, the road appears as an agger in Nine Acre Wood, and then along a minor road from Willow Wood.

From here, a minor road called "Roman Road" through Studdal and Roman Road Farm to Maydensole Farm marks the Roman road. South of this, the route is marked by a footpath, goes across a field at Napchester, then through Cane Wood near Pineham. The Roman road then runs along another footpath through Pineham to Barntye. From Maydensole Farm to Dover, the North Downs Way marks the Roman road. The route is then marked by a minor road near Buckland, and then it came into Dover, possibly along Frith Road and Bridge Street. It joined Watling Street (Margary's No. 1a) in Dover.

10.1. The Richborough to Dover Roman road as an agger in Ash.

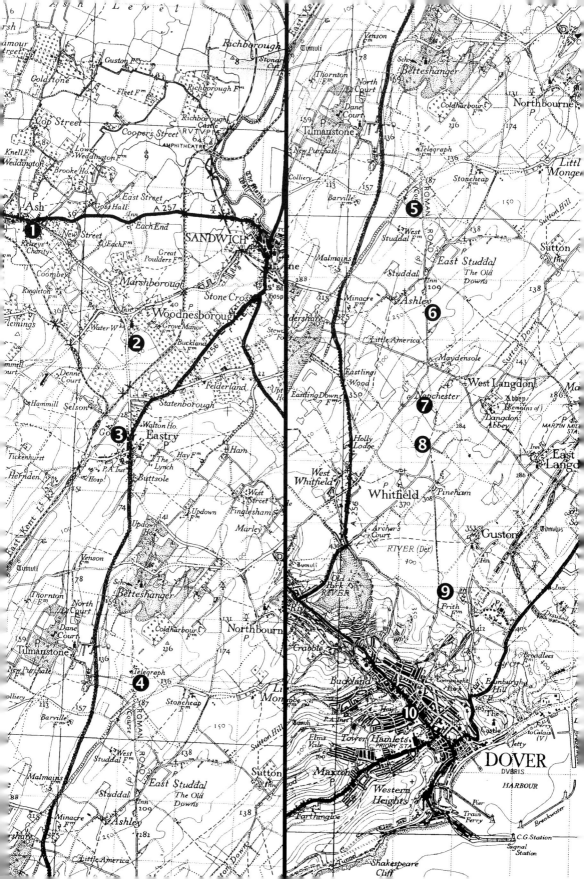

10.2. The route along Foxborough Hill in Woodnesborough.

10.3. The Roman road along the High Street through the village of Eastry.

10.4. The Roman road along a footpath at Telegraph Farm near Tilmanstone.

10.5. The route marked by a minor road at Willow Wood.

10.6. The road along Roman Road at Roman Road Farm, Studdal.

10.7. Site of the Roman road across a field at Napchester.

10.8. The Roman road marked by the North Downs Way at Cane Wood near Pineham.

10.9.   The route marked by the North Downs Way west of Frith Farm.

10.10. Possible line of the Roman road along Bridge Street in Dover where it joins Watling Street.

11. WOODNESBOROUGH TO SANDWICH
(101). 1 ½ miles

This short stretch of Roman road branched off the Richborough to Dover route (Margary's No. 100) at Woodnesborough just north of the church. It went in a north-easterly direction along a footpath from the church, and then along Sandwich Road east of Woodnesborough. From here, the Roman road is marked by another footpath near Stone Cross to Sandwich, where it goes to an estuary. There may have been a harbour at Sandwich in Roman times.

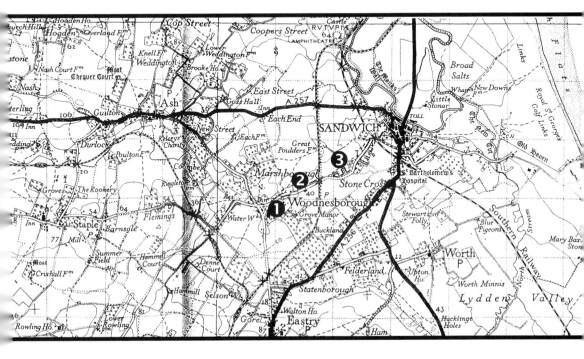

*11.1. The Woodnesborough to Sandwich Roman road marked by a
footpath in Woodnesborough.*

11.2. The route along Sandwich Road east of Woodnesborough.

11.3. The Roman road along a footpath near Stone Cross looking towards Sandwich.

12. STURRY TO RECULVER
(110). 5 ¾ miles

This Roman road branched off the Canterbury to Upstreet route (Margary's No 11) some ¾ mile east of Sturry. It ran along Babs Oak Hill and Hoath Road for about a mile or so to Stonerocks Farm and Hoades Court. After this, the road went east of the minor road where its course is marked by the edge of a wood from Tile Lodge Farm to Buckwell.

From here, the route ran along Maypole Road passing Rushbourne Manor, through Maypole near Hoath and Ford where it crossed a stream, went on a bend and over a hill. The Roman road continued along a minor road through Heart in Hand, Hawthorn Corner, Hillborough and then to Reculver. Here the Roman road entered the Roman fort of Regulbium at the south gate. It is possible that a Roman road entered the west gate going westwards to Herne Bay and beyond. This route would now be under the sea.

The Roman fort of Regulbium was built in 210 AD and became a Saxon shore fort in about 280 AD. The Wantsum Channel was a major shipping route at this time and the fort protected it. Today only the southern half of it exists with walls; the northern section was lost to the sea by coastal erosion. The ruins of the Saxon church of Reculver, with its twin towers, stands within the fort.

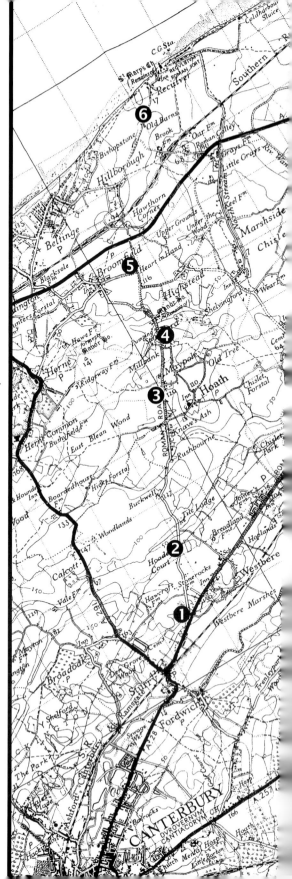

12.1.   The Sturry to Reculver Roman road along Babs Oak Hill in Sturry.

12.2.   The road along Hoath Road south of Tile Lodge Farm.

12.3. *The route along Maypole Road through Maypole near Hoath.*

12.4. *The Roman road along Ford Hill at Ford where it crossed a stream.*

12.5. The route along a minor road at Heart in Hand.

*12.6. The Roman road along Reculver Lane at Reculver where it entered the
Roman fort of Regulbium in the distance.*

13. BENENDEN TO CANTERBURY
(130). 28 ½ miles

This Roman road left the Rochester to Hastings route (Margary's No. 13) at Hempsted near Benenden, and went in a north-easterly direction to Canterbury via Ashford. There is very little evidence of the road to be seen today, but remains of iron slag and flint metalling is evident. It is marked by a lane west of St Michael's near Tenterden, to the north of a minor road at Pond Wood, along a treelined footpath at Tiffenden manor and to the south of a minor road at Plurenden.

East of Plurenden, the Roman road ran across a field, crossed a crossroads north of Great Engeham Manor, through Mayshaves north of a minor road, and through Herlakenden Farm. After this, the route is marked by footpaths at Snailswood Farm north of Shadoxhurst, (where there is an agger), and also at Stubb's Cross. North-east of Stubb's Cross, the road crossed the Maidstone to Dover Roman road (Margary's No. 131) at Stanhope west of Kingsnorth.

The route then went through Ashford along Beaver Road and the main A28. A footpath then marks it across a recreation ground in Kennington, (where there is a hollow way), an alleyway, and then a footpath to Kennington Hall. From here, the road is lost under a ploughed field and the A28 marks its course at Boughton Corner to Bilting. It then ran over Godmersham Downs to Godmersham where a lane marks it. After this, the Roman road turned to the east to cross the Great Stour River and then north again.

North of Godmersham, the Roman road is marked by footpaths, (using a pre-Roman trackway), from Chilham and over Julliberrie Downs and then over Chartham Downs. From here, the Roman road ran along Cockering Road from Shalmsford Street in Chartham to Thannington. After this, the A28 marks its course to the Worth Gate at Canterbury. It joined the Canterbury to Lympne Roman road (Stone street) some ½ mile out of the city. It is possible that this Roman road may have gone further west from Benenden to join the London to Lewes route (Margary's No. 14) possibly at Hartfield via Lamberhurst.

There were two branch roads of this Roman road at Tenterden, which went to an estuary. One of which came from the north-west to the south-east from Parkgate via Little Halden Place to the estuary. The other branched off the Roman road west of St Michael's, which ran north to south along a lane passing Coombe Farm, and then as a hollow across fields to the estuary north of Tenterden.

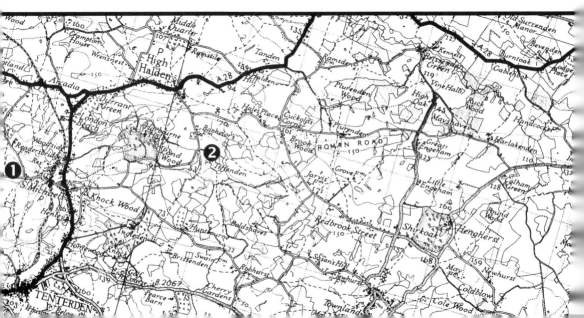

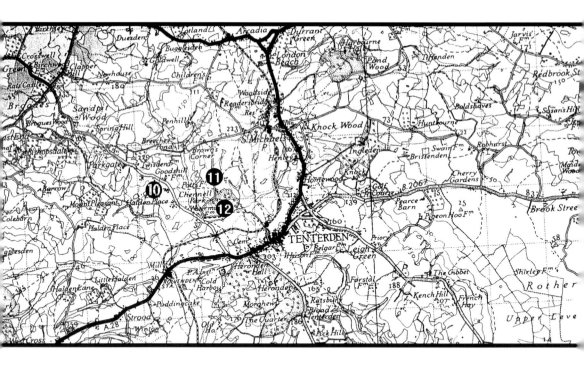

13.1. *The Benenden to Canterbury Roman road along a lane at St Michael's near Tenterden.*

13.2. The route marked by a treeline at Tiffenden.

13.3. Agger of the Roman road across a field at Snailswood Farm near Shadoxhurst.

13.4. Hollow way of the road across a recreation ground in Kennington.

13.5. The Roman road along a minor road, where it changes direction to cross the Great Stour River at Godmersham.

13.6. The route along a footpath on Julliberrie Downs near Chilham.

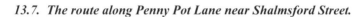

13.7. The route along Penny Pot Lane near Shalmsford Street.

13.8. The road along Cockering Road in Chartham.

13.9. The Benenden to Canterbury Roman road along the A28 in Canterbury.

13.10. Site of branch Roman road of the Benenden to Canterbury route in a valley near Halden Place.

13.11. Branch road of the Benenden to Canterbury Roman road at Coombe Farm.

13.12. Branch road of the Roman road as a hollow to an estuary north of Tenterden.

14. MAIDSTONE TO DOVER
(131). 35 ¾ miles

This Roman road left the Rochester to Hastings route (Margary's No. 13) at Amber Green and there is not much of it visible on its first part. It went in a south-easterly direction through Sutton Valence (where there is a terrace), Kingsnorth Wood, Woodsden and Vanden. It is then marked by a minor road at St Giles Farm near Pluckley, goes past Upper Coldharbour, and crosses the Benenden to Canterbury Roman road (Margary's No. 131) at Stanhope near Ashford.

From Ashford, the Roman road is marked by a footpath at Bilham Farm and then a minor road from Cheeseman's Green, South Stour and Broad Oak. It runs along Roman Road through Clap Hill and then Aldington, where there is a bend. After this, the road is marked by the B2067 from Postling Green near the site of old sea cliffs, through Court–at-Street to Lympne. At the latter place is the site of the Roman port and fort of Portus Lemanis to the south, which was served by the Canterbury to Lympne Roman road (Margary's No. 12), which crossed this one at Shepway Cross. From here, the Roman road continued along the B2067 and then a footpath south of Court Farm near Pedlinge to Hythe.

The section of this Roman road east of Hythe is uncertain, but a Roman road to Dover existed because one is indicated in the Peutinger Table, which is a diagrammatic road map of the 3rd century AD. It probably ran along North Road in Hythe and possibly turned north-east to Cheriton, and then along footpaths via Caesar Camp, Round Hill (a possible suggestive name), along Crete Road north of Folkestone, and through Capel le Ferne. From here it may have gone along footpaths to Church Hougham, over West Down to Stepping Down where it descended to the Roman town of Dubris in Dover.

It is possible that this Roman road went westwards from Maidstone to join the London to Lewes route (Margary's No. 14) at the Roman town of Noviomagus at West Wickham, possibly via Ightham and Otford. This would have provided a shorter London to Lympne (Portus Lemanis) route and also an alternative London to Dover route.

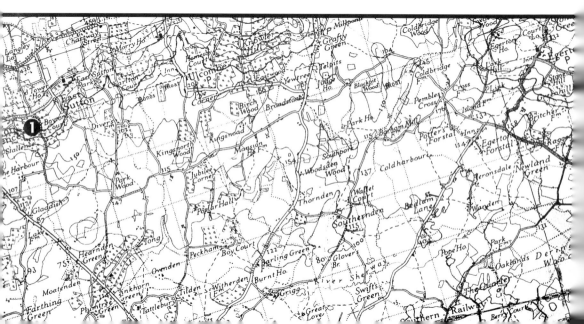

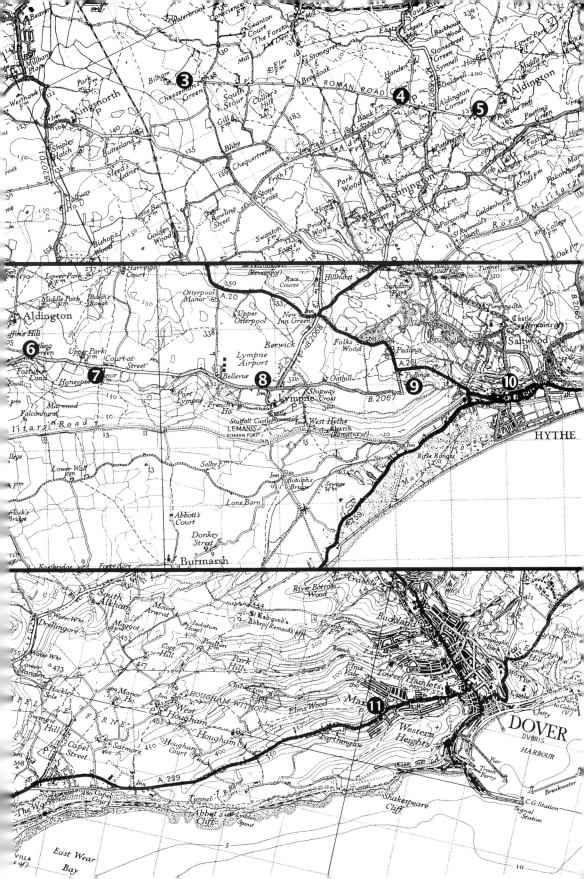

14.1. The Maidstone to Dover Roman road as a terraceway at Sutton Valence.

14.2. The route along a minor road at St Giles Farm near Pluckley.

14.3.   The road is marked by a track at Bilham Farm near Kingsnorth.

14.4.   The route along Roman Road through Clap Hill, Aldington.

14.5. *The road along a minor road at Aldington.*

14.6. The Roman road along the B2067 at the site of old sea cliffs at Postling Green.

14.7. The route along the B2067 through Court-at-Street.

14.8. The Roman road along the B2067 through Lympne.

14.9. The route marked by a footpath south of Court Farm near Pedlinge.

14.10. Possible line of the Roman road along North Road in Hythe.

14.11. Possible route of the Maidstone to Dover Roman road descending Stepping Down to the Roman town of Dubris in Dover.

15. OTHER ROMAN ROADS
AND TRACKS

There are other Roman roads still to be established in Kent, connecting existing roads and tracks. One of these is a newly discovered route (largely confirmed) going from the Roman town of Noviomagus at West Wickham on the London to Lewes Roman road (Margary's No 14), to Vagnacae at Springhead on Watling Street via Fordcroft and Darenth. Sections of the Roman road were found in West Wickham in 1966, Fordcroft in 1988, Darenth in 1969 and Springhead in 1963. It is possible that this Roman road went further west from West Wickham, possibly along a footpath and a hedgerow to the London to Brighton route (Margary's No.150) in the Croydon area.

Another possible Roman road is from Richborough to Reculver. This would have branched off the Canterbury to Richborough route at Fleet Farm and gone in a north-westerly direction, possibly along footpaths from here to Lower Goldstone, Paramour Street, Westmarsh, East and West Stourmouth. It then would have crossed the Wantsum Channel on a bridge, ferry or causeway to Upstreet (crossing the Canterbury to Upstreet Roman road) to Chislet, along a footpath and then a minor road to Highstead may mark its course via Boyden Gate. At Highstead, the Roman road would have gone along a footpath and joined the Sturry to Reculver route at Hillborough.

Another possible route is a branch road to the estuary at Sandwich. This would have left the Richborough to Dover Roman road at Ash, and run along the A257, and then a minor road at Each End where there is a bend. From here, it may have gone in a south-easterly direction to join the Woodnesborough to Sandwich Roman road at the estuary.

The number of trackways are too numerous to mention here, but one of them is the North Downs Ridgeway, which was a very ancient trackway and was probably used in Neolithic times or earlier. It goes from Wiltshire through to east Kent. It was used by the Romans, and one section of it became the Richborough to Dover Roman road (Margary's No. 100) between Studdal and Dover. Parts of the North Downs Ridgeway is known as "The Pilgrims Way", which is a name given to it in Medieval times for the Pilgrims who travelled along it from Winchester to Canterbury.

15.1. Possible route of the West Wickham to Springhead Roman road across a recreation ground in West Wickham.

15.2. Possible route of the West Wickham to Springhead route at the Roman town of Vagnacae at Springhead.

*15.3. Possible route of the Richborough to Reculver Roman road marked
by a footpath at Fleet Farm.*

15.4. Possible line of the Richborough to Reculver route along a footpath at Chislet.

15.5. Possible line of the Richborough to Reculver Roman road along a footpath at Highstead.

15.6 Possible route of the Ash to Sandwich Roman road at Each End, where there is a bend

15.7. The North Downs Way/Pilgrims Way along a country lane at Hognore Farm near Wrotham.